THE CHAOS OF DESIRE

THE CHAOS OF DESIRE

Poems by
Marin Bodakov

Translated by Katerina Stoykova

Accents Publishing • Lexington, Kentucky • 2024

Printed in the United States of America

Accents Publishing
Editor / Translator: Katerina Stoykova
Cover Image: *Beaumaris Mount, near Bangor, Wales* by William Collingwood

Library of Congress Control Number: 9781961127111
ISBN: 978-1-961127-11-1
First Edition

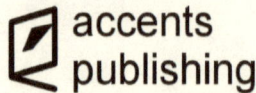

Accents Publishing is an independent press for brilliant voices. For a catalog of current and upcoming titles, please visit us on the Web at

www.accents-publishing.com

CONTENTS

INTRODUCTION

It was on the morning of September 8th, 2021, I woke up to devastating news from my home country of Bulgaria—Marin Bodakov had passed away. Wait. It can't be. Didn't he just turn 50? Weren't we the same age and I'm still alive? Didn't he have a full life, a wonderful family? Wasn't there more art for him to enjoy, examine and discuss? Didn't he have more books to write and publish?

But no, it was true, as much as I and all my literary friends didn't want it to be. He was one of the leading literary citizens in Bulgaria, and his passing sent the entire writing community into disbelief and mourning. I have never seen anything like this before or since. Everyone shared his poems and personal stories of kindnesses or services that Marin had done for them.

I also have a story with Marin Bodakov. We met in our teenage years, when we both started publishing poems in Bulgarian journals in the late 80s and early 90s. Even then, his style was recognizable—a few sparse words, each integral to building the structure of the poem. Nothing excessive or gratuitous. Yet somehow, the atomic cage of the poem unlocked something inside the reader—released the trapped energy of unsaid truths. That made Marin's work not only memorable, but also sought after. Over the course of his short life, he published eight collections of poems, from the first in his early twenties to the last, three years before his unexpected death.

In our twenties, our paths diverged sharply. I immigrated to the United States, and upon losing my connection with language and literary community, I suddenly stopped writing. Marin continued on the natural path of more reading, more writing and also—just as importantly— serving the field of poetry. It seemed to me that he read every book that was published in Bulgaria and beyond and was able to select a few to review for a column in a national newspaper. It was an honor to have your work reviewed by Marin Bodakov. He never missed a chance to lend a helping hand or state a socially engaged position, and also live it.

After 11 years of writers block, I started writing again and tried to re-emerge onto the Bulgarian literary scene. I wanted to share new work and read that of others. Marin Bodakov was the first person I contacted.

I asked him for advice on where to send my new poems. He almost immediately answered, pointing me to the right people. Over the years, he reviewed my books and spoke about them across a wide variety of media with no other motive but to share what he found exciting with the people who listened to his recommendations.

I wanted you to know what kind of person Marin Bodakov was before you go on to read this book and learn what kind of poet he is.

I am grateful to Marin's widow, writer and publisher Zornitsa Hristova, for granting me permission to select, translate and publish a collection of Marin Bodakov's poems in English. It was an honor to read through the entirety of his collected works and to immerse myself more deeply in the world of this remarkable poet. My hope is for *The Chaos of Desire* to find the right audience and for Marin Bodakov's words to reach readers with hearts open for beauty, love, service and uncompromising knowledge of self.

Katerina Stoykova

WHERE AM I

Which side of the battle do I stand on?
Years, felled, scattered all around.
Over there, the earth won't let me be.
Over here, the sky won't roll out a victory flag for me,
or even drop a noose made of snow.

EVERYWHERE

they wiped out the remaining animals of his species,
to increase the value
of his loneliness.

BEFORE I WAS BORN

in the mirror of a museum in Thessaloniki
I saw a block of ice

the unknown sculptor had chiseled only
the unpleasant profile of a young man
and the curls surrounding his penis

there are no reports on
what somber events suddenly prevented
the marble's choreography

there are no reports on the tedious,
insufficiently digested desires
that necessitated the widening of the aorta

inside the rock.

TO BE READ LITERALLY

large snowflakes
flitter through me
with words descending like entire poems
words disappearing above the heels
into the groin

AT NIGHT

between the river and the sea
only fishing poles without a catch
still glow.

FRIENDSHIP

Two pipes are filling a pool.
If the first one works for two hours,
it fills a third of the pool.
The second can fill it in three hours.
How many hours would it take—
for both pipes together—
to fill the pool of spring
with verdancy.

I CAN STILL SEE YOUR BREATH

The evergreen trees are verdant,
the deciduous ones—orange and red.
I'm dressed inappropriately.
Sometimes I catch up to you,
we exchange pleasantries about work.
With you, I become smarter than usual.
Your cheeks continue to hollow,
your pantlegs flap in the wind.
I lift my arm to point
toward your disappearance
and helplessly pull it back.

I feel you closer than ever,
and I don't want to talk.

I CAN STILL SEE YOUR BREATH

You stroll absentmindedly.
The evergreen trees are verdant, as always,
the deciduous ones—already orange and red.
I'm dressed inappropriately.
Sometimes I catch up to you,
we exchange pleasantries about work.
With you, I become smarter than usual.
Your cheeks continue to hollow,
your pantlegs start flapping in the wind.
I lift an arm, try to point to where your stomach has disappeared,
and bring it back. I feel you closer than ever,
I have less and less to tell you,
and you withdraw.

EMBRACE

Before I realized it, I crossed
into the conquered enemy camp,
finding myself among those tasked
with removing ornaments from the Christmas tree—
cautiously, one by one.

That's why I quit inquiring
about the appropriate length of a hug
and what prolongs it—desperation or desire.
(You know, you detach from another's chest,
and seconds later you attach again, in place of goodbye.)

That's why I wake up every night—to be alone, at least for a bit,
to have nothing looming or urgent to do;
a Christmas tree, embraced in panic on the way to the dumpster,
a needle, unswept from the floor.

THE CHAOS OF DESIRE

What do I transport in your embrace,
what do I smuggle?
Chaos, which pronounces the unpronounceable,
desire, which bears the unbearable,
counterfeit treasures.

The body withdraws, becomes weightless.
The body pulsates.

* * *

From you I beg forgiveness,
dear body.

Silence grows
over your enchanting parts,
death infuses you
with shyness.

Let's make peace
while we're still here.

A STRIKE

I cannot recall at all
what the knees were doing,
the dawn at the abdomen—was it yours or mine,
were the toes wiggling,
did the veins crackle …

… in the mindfolds—only dry kindling,
just kindling.

THE NEW SENTIMENTALITY

How did I manage to succeed
without the peaceful passenger blanket
and the shy rations of dreams,
without the splurge of memories?

Embryos of fog float above the paper,
the smoke thickens into pills and ointments,
a pinch of anxiety shatters home's comfort—
why this game, precisely?

I won through absentmindedness,
my stupidity wholly flummoxed the opponent.
And today I sense the real confrontation elsewhere.

WITH ALTERED VOICE

How should we measure
the braking distance of emotion:
in meters, months?

The absent one fiercely flosses
between the words of the other.

I'VE NEVER SEEN IT AT NIGHT,

but I waited to remain alone
and kissed the lock on the lighthouse.
"A lock," you'd say.
"A lighthouse," I'd add.
And we'd all be right.

This is a

THWARTED POEM,

forever derailed from the course of its genuine words.
In it I was going to relate
how at one point I tucked my sandals into a backpack,
and shamelessly barefoot, kept getting off the ship—island after island—
while on my heels the dust of cozy ports blended.
And when—at last, yet fast—we arrived at the place
that takes nine years to reach,
a prideful expert in cliché tried to shake our confidence:
"His kingdom is actually
in the place you departed from;
this island is too small to be both your kingdom and his."
He did not realize that on my heels
all islands already lived happily together.

TO GRETZ, AGAINST TIME

1

In the blistering temple
of my last years,
the young man I wanted to be
calmly enters with his dogs
and doesn't notice me at all.
A friendship rains, then stops,
the breeze of light stirs the blossoms,
here and there the destitute pray.
Keep quiet is posted everywhere,
but the child can't read yet.

2

Not the silence, but its prospect
switches the perspective sharply—
fear swallows its gut and looks better,
still life turns into a landscape,
vases and potted plants loom above me,
the bottles are towers, the empty boxes—cathedrals.
By the way, these are the same heavy pots of evergreens
that a certain woman, otherwise exceedingly absentminded,
straightens out with a flair, without forethought,
whenever a fierce rain topples them
into my courtyard.

3

The windows are open
and one can hear everything:
hunger ripens into manhood
and scribbles its first creations,
a stranger living next door
drops a piece of bread under the table,
and I will have to eat it.

AUTUMN ARRIVED,

the anchors and the trees mixed,
the infants disturb the abstract sermon,
the orderlies start washing the stretchers on the hour,
the ambulances crash for no reason,
the houses appear emptier than us.
I mash *yes* and *no* between my fingers—and blend them,
Even though this isn't yet a medicine.

* * *

Is this Summer?
Chatting with Love in a third language—
neither yours, nor Love's.
Wandering a cemetery of a distant country—
strangers cuddling.
Masts between the huts, the fence—crumpled in the grass.
A village angel mending your shoes nearby,
what's the rush?

MY WIFE,

my future wife
walks behind the beauty of December.
A piece of pine forest glows in her embrace,
the sea lays siege to us, it's a holiday.

In her lap's contours I divine
the uncertain indications of a child.
I abandon mixed feelings.

In the atria—the left and the right,
among the chambers—the right and the left,
joy calmly settles back,
breath thunders.

SHALLOW VEIN

It rides along the ellipse of the neck—
not large, but wide enough
to freely let through
blue skies and green grass,
trailed by the breathing of beautiful babies
and blood clots of eternity.
This shallow vein—
the only jewelry
worthy of you.

CHRISTMAS SONG

(For the second morning in a row I find a potato
in the holiday stocking.)
I must reach the sea,
lean the bicycle on the sharp rocks,
as you had done the year before.
You—the light above my name, the wave inside it
with two baby fish.

POCKET GARDEN

The melancholy assesses,
steps back, squints:
which branches of the bush of words to clip,
so in springtime they will sprout
on their own

THE LAKE WITH THE LILIES

in the morning I skip with the balloons
subtle fog descends in circles

by nighttime barking has felled
every lily

* * *

four kings
perished in my battle
there is no more north or east,
nor west nor south
life seems tilted
yet does not collapse

just the star of air
slaps me on the mouth

ROOSTER AND FISH

My secret
is a festive golden rooster above the fog.
When constantly spinning, it directs everyone
to the source of the chill.

GROWING SENSE OF DEPARTURE

I surfaced
with a ballad on my mind:
An elderly couple at the market,
We cannot afford this apple, sweetheart—
and they walk on with dignity.

STILL LIFE WITH WAX

they don't sense the catastrophe:
they don't turn towards Icarus
nor towards me

nor do they suspect a difference between the two of us

ADDITION TO A POEM

In addition to the two pink feet
outlining the greedy beak of death,

upon peering at the original, one can make out
the hand of Icarus.

Sore comb for the labyrinth of waves,
five fingers grasp the absurd support of water;
a detail not subject to reproduction.

Then four fingers.
Then three.

HUNGRY MILK

Without a declared competition,
the winner is proclaimed.
Production quality immaterial,
jury competency irrelevant:
the award for best supporting role
always goes to death.

Someone else's, of course.

HALF A DEATH

Fall arrives
with the speed at which
the just-peeled eggplant darkens,
arrives in the red onion of the eye.
Fall arrives with the retort of an old friend:
"At least we could have gotten in a fight
instead of you falling alone."

HORRIFIED FASCINATION

The feet—
lowered toward the floor. The gurney—
a trampoline above the empty pool of the past.

One by one, the musicians vacate
the philharmonic of his breath—
quartet, trio, duet with the wife.

On departure, stunned, he notices
that his emaciated ass has left a crimson track on the sheet.
He's not the only one surprised.

A contest of silences before the examination;
the surgeon finds no hemorrhages.
Years with neither life nor death are at hand.

Then at the museum I see an installation:
Hospital hallway. A pale boy with his face averted is trailed
by drops of blood. There is no wound.

I see my Dad.

A JABBERING MONSTER

the awakening
rips open the bag of my dreams

a phrase grows in my plowed head,
mine, a quote of no consequence:
"childhood is a secret compartment where a garden is hidden"

another night:
I drive toward me,
crash into my three-year-old self,
the boy is bleeding, the tricycle overturned,
three wheels calmly turn in the air
I continue straight through the gardens

third night of insomnia:
I'm waiting for my father's death, so I can be with my child

FLUID LIGHT

       he considered the community
        and the attempt to die in place of another

I'm sitting on a bench, rubbing the stress point
of my bared heel

I've taken the first grader to school,
more Turner clouds remain
until my first lecture in the university

today one can see the light
whooshing between the skin and the clothes
of the runners,

the liquid granite of the Perlovska river,
the white shirts above the shifting carpet of fall leaves,
and more

       I'd like to die in place of autumn
       I write to you as an answer

BEGINNING OF SUMMER

I announced the death to completely random people
along with repugnant details—
I could quickly dismiss them,
chase away their dreadful manners.

My loved ones suspect nothing:
every caring touch mimics a casual gesture,
purposely illustrates someone else's action.
(Just my breastbone disappeared.)

FINAL DRAFT

now we're dressing the corpse
and having issues with the buttons

now we're readying the corpse
and sniffing shadows in the air

now we're carrying out the corpse
and covering it with dirt and branches

we sense a lack of organs
with which to mourn

at this moment

MUD ON MY PALM

Under the rain and out of patience,
rain from May's water and dirt,
in the company of a curious dog,
but left without supervision,
they hadn't entirely finished.
On the next day, we discovered the greasy dirt waist-high,
wet dirt heaped under the bench, outside at his feet,
there was no other way, with my little garden shovel,
I finished burying my dad.
I wish this were a metaphor.

(I DREAM THAT I COVER THE GRAVE WITH WET BLANKETS)

my father's corpses—
no irresponsible copies, only originals,
many bodies of the same old man—
stretching everywhere around my home,
face down

(I DREAM THAT I'M DANCING)

two men,
elderly father and elderly son
dance a tango—
and the father drags the son toward the sidewalk
in mute music

A CHILDREN'S BOOK IN AN UNFAMILIAR LANGUAGE

What kind of soup did my father like as a child,
did he clean his plate,
what did he hide under the big pillow,
at what word in the story did he fall asleep,
did the bombings truly frighten him.
I'll never learn any of this,
my fatherland has been irrevocably lost.
The air is so desolate
that I clearly hear the schedule of the train station
and the harbor siren embraces me.

RECOGNITION

dawn brightens after eight
dusk arrives before three
the abs of sleep are flat
in this place
the book
supplies the light

I ONLY KNOW HOW TO SAY THANK YOU IN THIS LANGUAGE

and that's more than enough.
Took me too long to grasp
that thank you is a synonym for all words in all languages
and has no antonyms at all.

HE WRITES

malnourished poems.
Words' shoulder blades stick out, pierce the skin,
though they continue grazing his chest
and sweetly kicking.

PREPARING FOR A READING

This one is too sexy and suggestive.
This one they'll understand literally.
This precedes the correct choices.
This one they'll use to blackmail me.
I won't share the next one either.

I WRITE AT THE PLACES FROM WHICH ONE GROWS,

those places with pale and diluted beauty
that take another's thought-pajamas off mine.
The warm fur on me grows and grows,
covers mysterious stitches even my mother can't recall,
a wisdom tooth sprouts in my mouth,
so useless for these places.

* * *

Falling asleep you have a tooth,
waking up—you don't. You've eaten it.
This goes on night after night.

Until
your tongue remains utterly alone,
like a forgotten streetlamp
left on during daylight.

TONIGHT, TOO

I stuttered uncontrollably.
Disjoined, identical syllables
kept pouring from my mouth:
"I want to live my own life."
That's exactly what I wanted to say.

Then, behind the trash can
I secretly ate food I'd cast deep into it,
and covered up and forgotten.

ONLY SILENCE WON'T BETRAY YOU—

the way the weary master won't abandon his elderly servant;
only silence will teach you to sleep with the door open
and expect nothing.

MATURITY BROUGHT NOTHING—

only toppled chairs, wrinkled laundry.
And at the end, as a saving grace—
fewer secret rendezvous,
more secret breakups.

CERTAIN GOODBYES RESEMBLE

a stain on a tablecloth.
You drag the plate to cover it
before the other notices.
That's all you think about.

TWO LIVES

To keep myself honest,
more and more often I answer, "I don't know."
I put amazement away
with the laundry detergent,
humility—with the knives.

PASSING MANIFESTO

So many wars
where all opposing parties appeal to you
to side with them,
to arm yourself with their outrage,
to adopt their fears.
So many dirty wars
lacking redeeming heroes—
just righteous ones you can barely catch up with.
As many shameful, fake wars,
as all these masterful attempts to derail you
from your own tiny, pathetic war,
from the shrapnel of the buttercup and the munition of the crocus,
to forget that you shoot only towards the sky—
and never against people.

To forget why you are striding stooped towards the lighthouse,
since you have no ship.

* * *

Two knives—
each against one of the sides
that once I wanted to reconcile.
Those knives I later threw out the window,
although sleep was in my way.
Because there is no need
for battling insanity and stupidity,
nor for choosing between wrong and wrong.
But even though I set the weapons aside,
I continue wounding.

AFFECTION

I remember that person,
his wound like a ship,
his ship like a blanket,
his blanket like a swamp,
the swamp like a star.
A person like a person.

* * *

Guileless sky—
turns sins into mistakes,
wine into water.
Me into you.

THREE ACTS AND A CURTAIN

I need a snorkel.

Nobody responds.

He erases the request.

A DRILL

This day, too:
like a lily with no name,
like a shovel with no grave.
Like a priest with no God.

There is no earth for the snow to fall upon,
It's just falling.

HERE

Mislead by heatwaves,
I leave the tourist zone of unhappiness
and the locals recognize me as a foreigner,
even though I was born here—right here.

THERE

My childhood has been demolished,
built up with ruins, new shopping malls,
hotels putting on airs,
houses imitating relics, weeds.
The squatters do not recognize me,
and if they speak, they muddle my language.

If you'd like to purchase a cheap property in my childhood,
I have no connection to this address.

★ ★ ★

Next to my childhood home
a Museum of Illusions was opened.

Why are you by yourself,
certain illusions need a couple,
normally I don't allow people on their own,
invite someone to accompany you.

LIKE THIS TOWER

Needlessly reworked
throughout the years
(and considerably shorter than before),
for some time now it hasn't been a lighthouse,
nor barracks, nor modest chapel,
there are no knights.

And you alone tend to the humble museum
with no visitors.

UNMAILED LETTER

I went to the executioner's house,
which utilizes the last surviving partition of the fortress's wall.
You know, those stones were pillaged
so we could build spacious mansions,
so you could discuss with the steward the menu for the inaugural ball,
how best to light the stoves,
so I could calculate the next business deal while playing solitaire
and waiting for dinner.
By the way, the executioner turned out to be a really nice man,
I stayed all day to pester him.
I didn't allow him to get any work done,
I am yet to leave.

TROLLEY #2

On the seat next to me
a three- to four-year-old angel
wearing an ushanka hat
has kept on asking this question
for the last few stops:

Daddy, why won't you talk to me?
Daddy, why won't you talk to me?
Daddy, why won't you talk to me?

Then leans his forehead on the glass—and so
nearly two millennia pass.
The trolley reaches their stop,
Daddy silently stretches out a hand,
they get off.

I—and, forgive me, humanity—
remain in our seats.

ABOUT THE AUTHOR

Marin Bodakov was a Bulgarian poet, essayist, critic, journalist and editor who made significant contributions to the Bulgarian literary community, both with his recognizable poetic style and with his long-term service to the literary life of the country.

Born in the town of Veliko Tarnovo, Bulgaria on the 28th of April, 1971, Marin studied Bulgarian Philology at St. Kliment Okhridski University in Sofia, where he earned a Ph.D. and taught creative writing to several generations of young writers. Between 2000 and 2018, Marin was a book review columnist in the national journal *Kultura*. His column, "Walking on Letters," could be called a chronicle of the publications and releases of notable books in Bulgaria during this time period.

Marin Bodakov is the author of nine volumes of poetry, most recently *The Gallery of the Heart: Collected Poems*, published jointly by DA and Tochitsa in 2022. His book, *Naïve Art* won the Ivan Nikolov national book award for 2012. In 2014 he received the Knight of the Book Prize from The Association of the Bulgarian Book. In 2021 and 2022 he was given two posthumous awards for his cumulative contributions to the Bulgarian literary environment.

He is survived by his wife, translator, writer and publisher Zornitsa Hristova, and their two daughters.

ABOUT THE TRANSLATOR

Katerina Stoykova is the author of several award-winning poetry books and the Senior Editor of Accents Publishing, where she has selected, edited, and published close to 80 poetry collections. Katerina acted in the lead roles in the independent feature films *Proud Citizen* and *Fort Maria*, both directed by Thom Southerland. She splits her time between the coast of the Black Sea and the rolling hills of Kentucky. Katerina writes, lives and thinks in two languages.